Simple wisdoms:

Individuals and society

By Stephen B. Waters

Printed in the United States of America

Waters, Stephen B.

Simple Wisdoms: Individuals and Society/ Stephen B. Waters
ISBN-13: 978-0-9845258-4-3 (Paperback)

Library of Congress Control Number: 2023903621

File under Social Sciences in popular libraries and under philosophy in academic libraries.

Published by:
Stephen Waters
6391 Karlen Rd.
Rome, NY 13440

Dedication

To Bryce and Ayden, that they may stand taller on the shoulders of those who have gone before.

Acknowledgements

To my wife, Wendy, brilliant in her own right, while at the same time warm, loving, nurturing as any natural teacher should be. She puts up with me although, as God is my witness, I don't know why!

To my blogging friends at Just One Minute and JOM2, for their intellectual and social counterpoint. Let me especially single out Clarice Feldman, blog commenter and columnist whose keen legal eye and writing clarity nail so many issues to the page.

To our newspaper, the family-owned Rome (NY) Daily Sentinel and its past, present, and future publishers who have recognized the importance of local news for community cohesion. And to Rome, NY, itself, because it has been an oasis of humanity in which to raise wonderful children and grandchildren.

To all those across history on whose shoulders I stand. Thank you.

Regards/Stephen

Table of Contents

Where society begins

The most significant threat our country has ever faced is the attempt to invert the structure of America to become, not bottom-up governance, but top-down rule.

Individuals need community because they are fallible, so they create community. Accordingly, the individual is, and ought to be, the keystone of community.

Each of us is alone. Even when interacting together, we are alone. Recognizing that helps clear cobwebs that for millennia have confused attempts to organize society with others. Each person is insular and unique, with his or her own history, obliged to make decisions from uniquely personal experience. You can never hug anyone close enough that they can make those decisions for you.

Likewise, when it comes to encouraging society with others, none of us can depend on institutions overtaken by rust, as have been many schools, universities, news businesses, cultural institutions, churches, and even families.

Complicating the issue, language often confuses reasoning. People often overlook that people across history have created words to represent their thoughts. Sometimes those words have represented more than one thought. As time progressed, new words were created to separate the different meanings of original words. More recently, a trend known as postmodernism purposely trashed the common meanings of words to obscure and confuse. It's a way to lie, and people need to recognize how significant are the consequences of those lies.

Society

In Aristotle's time, one of the slippery words was *polis*, commonly translated as "society." Sociologists suggest a society is any group with common territory, interaction, and culture. In their quest for impartiality, their definition overlooks that it is individuals who create society for their own and for mutual benefit.

Society that acts uncivil does not become a different form of society. Instead it turns away from society altogether, reverting back to the wild where people compete under the Law of the Jungle—a realm of no rules where nothing matters but strength, speed, cunning, and luck.

Complicating the arrangement, society is often undermined by those who wrongly believe society-warping chaos is theirs to create, manipulate, and mine, even as they isolate themselves from the consequences of their own actions.

At its basic, every individual is responsible for guarding the society to which they belong and from which they benefit. Individuals share the responsibility to call out where society needs repair or they cede control to barbarians of ignorance and the new dark age they risk.

It's you, because that's how preserving society was meant to be from the beginning. Previous generations failed for a number of reasons. They did not shoulder the responsibility to revalidate principles passed down to succeeding generations. The question was how to do so. The generations gave in to "Trust the leaders," "Because I said so," "Peace is the answer," "Whatever," or "The other side is evil" and failed to reinforce that the responsibility always has been individual.

Forming society

Society is created at an edge where any two individuals or cultures meet. Creating society requires no religion, no shared experience, and no natural law, although they may be peripheral. Society is built projecting forward, in an exercise like two ships on a storm-tossed sea in times of need. One ship uses uses a Lyle Gun to shoot a messenger line to the second ship that then uses the first "messenger line" to return a stronger line. The process is repeated until the ships are lashed together.

A verbal messenger line sent between individuals or cultures must be constructed so it can travel across language, culture, time, and distance. It must be strong enough that the individuals can fashion a sturdy fabric to stand independent of their cultures, to lift them ever so slightly above the rest of the animal kingdom and to embrace a peaceful process of problem resolution.

This calls for individuals to understand enough about themselves that they can either invent the messenger line, or validate proposed lines others recommend.

Society differs from culture

The claim that natural right does not exist is irrelevant when deductions from experience and projections from them can create a safer and more useful environment in which to move forward. As explained in Socratic dialog in my 2010 *Individuals, Journalism, and Society*:

"But is it practical?"

"You need no more proof than your own experience. Governance with institutionalized doubt has been tried in one form or another in ancient Greece and today."

"They were not successful then."

"Those governments were instituted for other reasons and when they fell they were undermined by the lack of understanding of its underlying advantage."

"Then why were they instituted?"

"Instituted as a check on consolidated power in Athens, their faith in democracy was based on one person—one vote and majority rules. Instead, the strength of democracy is that it codifies humility into a permanent appreciation that there might be a better way. It represents a commitment to freedom of speech because the least of us deserves the opportunity to convince the rest that, whatever the present decision, there may always be a better way."

"Democracies are susceptible to tyranny of the majority and to buying votes for political advantage."

"Every form of government can become tyrannical. In a democracy, the capacity to make individual decisions matters. Democracy assures the ability to call "bullshit" in front of an audience tuned to judge the accuracy of the argument. Brought to consciousness by the charge, individuals choose to laugh into submission one side or the other. And, in the end, the penalty for bullshit ought to be to be ignored."

Furthermore, such understandings are not anti-religion, insofar as for many religions, they may fit hand in glove. Later in the book:

"Faith is critical to religion."

"But what are the limits of faith? If a charismatic leader like Jim Jones in Jonestown, Guyana, decides that you are to drink poisoned Kool-Aid, on what basis would you oppose him? If followers of a religion decide that you must convert to their worldview, on what basis would you oppose them? Where religion is misused by charismatics to consolidate power, who but you is in a position to declare what you see?"

"What do you do when faith conflicts with faith?"

"Welcome to the multi-cultural world where, finding no answer, others would avoid the question."

"The quest for religious uniformity is equally fraught with error."

"Enforced diversity is as demeaning, dysfunctional, and divisive as enforced unity. Celebrate individuality and diversity but avoid moral relativism. Prof. John Schmidt relates that German Enlightenment philosopher Moses Mendelssohn recognized that none of us thinks like our fellow man, so we should not deceive ourselves that we do. He warned that attempting to unify religion does not create unity. It imposes equality at the expense of liberty and prevents diversity that constantly works to find a better way.

"Mendelssohn's friend, playwright Gotthold Lessing, explained in Nathan the Wise, the parable of the man blessed with the ring of God. The man had two identical rings made and gave the rings to his three sons who asked which of the three was the true ring. The only proof was in the practice. What makes me for you a Christian makes you for me a Jew or Muslim. But it is what they share and what differentiates them that is worth celebrating. Specific religions matter less than the humanity they sponsor."

The sweep of history

The last several centuries provide ample evidence that different ruling styles have left other problems for their successors. We have yet to find the most workable blend. We are at a pivot point in how people choose to see the world. As each new century attempted to climb out of the mess left by the previous century, and to avoid the mistakes of the past, it destined itself to make new and greater mistakes.

The 1500s ended with the awareness that organized religion had simply become politics by another name. Reaction to that fostered the rise of humanistic awareness of the world around us—consider Francis Bacon, Cervantes, Shakespeare, and Galileo.

In the 1600s, religious wars of the previous century were supplanted by absolutist rulers in the hope that would lead to a better, more stable society. However, even then Whigs were objecting to bureaucrats' usurpation of political power. Along the way, rudimentary science, art, and philosophy offered a foothold for the secular empire in the century to follow. For that, consider Bacon again, René Descartes, Thomas Hobbes, and John Locke.

When secular autocratic empires of the 1600s didn't live up to expectations, the 1700s represented the next great hope that science and reason would overcome superstition, prejudice, and dogma and would lead to a better society. Intellects that blossomed then included Edmund Burke, Denis Diderot, Moses Mendelssohn, David Hume, Voltaire, Immanuel Kant, and Adam Smith.

When reason proved not enough, the 1800s turned to industry and to commerce as the next great hope for better society. It turned out that, while education matters, facts and reason were not enough. Hegel championed human will but Arthur Schopenhauer warned people not to forget their hidden drives.

By the 1900s, superstition, prejudice, and dogma fought back, consolidating power using clichéd notions to drive the masses.

Opportunists harnessed communications, technology, and social institutions to grab for power in a way the great hope became the great hype. Chaos, it turns out, is not enough and neither is regimented schooling. The 20th century deserves to be called the pathetic century. It became known for consolidation of both industry and governments into large institutional dinosaurs. Ironically, the election of 2008 was not to be the beginning of hope and change for the new century, but the last wheeze of spent dogma recycled from decades earlier.

The new century—the 21st—represents the small hope that individuals can reach sufficient awareness about themselves to inoculate themselves against usurpers in ways that might necessarily lead to better society.

Natural law

Dr. Robert Kraynak, Colgate University (Hamilton, NY) Political Science professor and Director of the Center for Freedom & Western Civilization, suggested the problem faced by American Founding Fathers:

> Without natural law—meaning, an objective moral law inscribed in nature and human nature by the Creator—the ideal of republican liberty lacks an ultimate foundation.[1]

While the solution of the founders was remarkable, the explanation to citizens provided no proof. The succeeding two centuries were bumpy in part because "natural law" can only be read and understood through our own experience, checked and rechecked by intellectual skills developed over time from Aristotle to the present day.

While the liberty embodied in the republican constitution was justified by a universal ideal of justice rooted in the moral order of the universe, not merely created by man, its substance was not made clear. The Declaration of Independence asserts that our liberty and

---

[1] https://isi.org/modern-age/the-american-founders-and-their-relevance-today/

rights come from "the laws of nature and of nature's God," but that is an assertion, not a derivation.

If "all men are created equal" and possess certain inalienable rights, it may be the case that the Creator put them in human nature and created a natural universe with a rational moral order, but it is up to us make that case accessible to any with the ability to grasp it, for our own safety's sake. Principles need to be expressed such that mastering the logic of the principles makes them accessible and compelling.

While people have similar tools, their capacity to use them is different. Confucius called the natural law required for society with others *li* in Chinese or "The Way" in English. He divided people into three groups according to their ability to grasp "The Way."

- Saints, his first group, intuitively understood "The Way."
- The second group, in which he included himself, could learn "The Way."
- The last group, absent the skill to grasp and validate "The Way" for themselves, he advocated fixed laws and rules to follow.

The Law of the Jungle applies those who choose not to follow laws. Individuals in society are forced to defend themselves against those who, by their actions, demonstrate an unwillingness or inability to fit into the respect those groups created.

Individuals learn from their own experience

Some recent philosophers have suggested morality is relative and therefore ineffective for organizing society. Morality is not relative if views are expressed in a framework that others recognize hold equally valid for them, even if separated by culture, language, time and distance.

People are like ships, alien and alone on uncertain seas. Every individual is essentially adrift in a stormy sea of sense experience, with only the pattern-recognition skills with which one was born and whatever rationality developed over time. Nevertheless, a sufficiently stable framework to work together can be deduced from one's own personal experience.

First, we have the ability to think about our own thinking. Many don't recognize or label recursive thinking or recursion. Nevertheless, useful lessons spring from the practice. Recall how often in your past you thought you were right and later, to your regret, discovered you were mistaken. In 1585, Montaigne wrote:

> If a man remembers how very many times he has
> been wrong in his judgment, will it not be foolish
> of him not to mistrust it ever after?

Most people can recall such an event from their own personal experience. Hubris—the excessive, unjustified pride where you think you are right simply because you believe you are right—collapses under the realization that you have previously been wrong.

Humility and humanity spring from realizing such personal limitations. If one can't know when one might be mistaken, any plan for the very best future requires a mental map be more accurate than an individual alone likely can make. This awareness is the "messenger line" individuals can use to nudge others to build society with them.

Humility matters

Any stable framework must spring from personal sense experience because that is the only experience with which one has to work. Your individual framework has the potential to mesh with frameworks others have created from their own personal experience. Such frameworks, while neither absolute nor universal, might as well be because they exist and function as if they were.

Other key concepts form principles that also are invariably accessible from personal experience:

- A sense that one can think about one's thinking using a dynamic recursive process.
- A sense that one might sometimes be wrong.
- A sense that one's mental map of reality could be more accurate.
- A sense that others live their lives as acutely — as consciously — as you live yours.

Simple Wisdoms: Individuals and Society

- A sense of time and one's place in it.
- A sense that individuals are responsible for themselves.

Humility pushes individuals outside themselves to form society with others who can add new and useful input. In that humility, people begin to value society with others, and join with them to check each individual's mental map of reality. Individual understanding, along with economic advantage, compels social cohesion.

In 1831, Japanese ukiyo-e artist, Hokusai, carved a woodblock print called "The Great Wave off Kanagawa." It visualizes how individuals, cast adrift in storm-tossed waves of sense experience, can find greater stability if they lash together with others.

Another visual representation of individuals in society, consists of three concentric circles. The innermost represents individuals, while the outermost represents the society that individuals create with each other. Individuals also create a middle circle that represents journalism to help join the other circles together.

Society

Journalism

Individuals

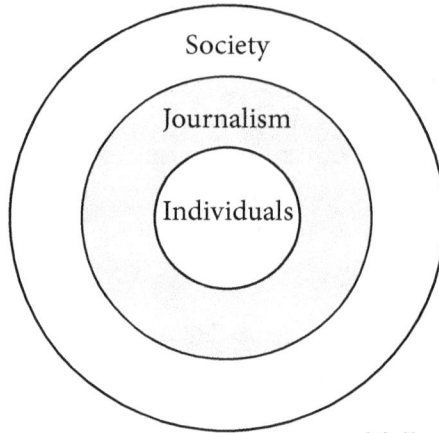

Individuals, journalism, and society are interrelated. What is important to one circle is important for the others. Defects in any one circle, affect the others. One circle not held accountable warps the others. That relationship forms the foundation to deduce the principles needed to wisely interact.

Reciprocity matters

Reciprocity is another fundamental principle besides humility. It acknowledges that you as an individual live life as acutely—as consciously—as others do. They, too, can consciously make decisions that affect the quality of their own lives and deserve to make those decisions using the most solid information available.

No individual is inherently superior to any other. Just as one needs others to represent themselves accurately, those others want everyone else to represent things accurately to them. If one discovers others misrepresent themselves—if they lie—one feels cheated and angry that they show no respect.

It follows that, since every individual deserves a sound map of reality upon which to operate, substantive lies in society are unacceptable. A liar chooses to misrepresent reality. A liar doesn't think clearly. A liar doesn't respect your need to have an accurate mental map with which to make decisions. Neither does that liar respect society or himself. Those who support liars lie to themselves. Liars undermine relationships among individuals. Too much political activity today is based on lies, or at least incomplete representations. Peripherally, those who take "offense" at others who tell them the truth play a postmodern rhetorical game constructed to undermine interaction with others.

That which is important to the individual is equally important both to journalism and society. Developing the skill to detect bad journalistic misbehavior is equally valuable for individuals and society. Current unacceptable journalistic habits that pervert civic interaction include selective use of facts, omission of pertinent facts, innuendo, "gotcha" techniques, style over substance, ignorance, misuse of statistics, gullibility, historical amnesia, double standards, misrepresentation, misplaced tolerance, misplaced judgment, silence, politics, overused and underused language, rhetorical games, and logical fallacies.

Equivalent tactics apply to individuals communicating with each other. After all, the purpose of a discussion is not to win, but to come to understanding.

Deduced principles matter

H. L. Mencken, perhaps the most astute political reporter during the major expansion of American government in the 20th century, observed, "The urge to save humanity is almost always a false front for the urge to rule it." At that time, politicians who pushed for expansion claimed to be principled and altruistic. Looking back, their principles were beliefs and their altruism served themselves more than anyone else.

Principles spring from personal experience crosschecked with experiences outside your own. People also forge principles from threads of wisdom drawn from historical experience that are distilled across time, vetted in the fiery crucible of thought, and then tested by projecting their application across possible futures to estimate potential consequences.

Not so rigorously tested are attitudes, beliefs, qualities, and standards that have not been forged across history or revalidated by each succeeding generation of individuals to the point they become logically compelling. Values may be processes or goals that come out of that. They appear the result of applying principles. It's easy to get confused trying to sift principles, values, attitudes, habits, and beliefs to deduce those that form the core from which all others follow.

When you master principles, understanding makes them compelling. They master you. Once understood, principles become rock-solid and a wellspring of courage and purpose.

The current state of affairs

Today people face elite leaderships that claim moral and intellectual high ground without providing evidence. The power elite posture a better world that masks a world fashioned just for them. The current common background is one of lies made and tolerated.

Unwilling or unable to muster the intellectual effort required to regularly revalidate principles that form and maintain society, they give up the process, and bluff their way ahead. They resign themselves to Machiavellian rule, despite historical evidence that sooner or later that path was guaranteed to inflict serious damage on themselves, their families, and their friends. They know what is coming, which makes what they do not just shortsighted, but also criminal. Furthermore, even Machiavelli understood that the goal of governance in a free republic was to successfully manage conflict.

For the most part, in their selfishness, the power elite do not care about your humanity— that you live your life as acutely and consciously as they live theirs. They do not care about their place in time and what the future will bring. They do not care that they abuse language to confuse people. They do not care what institutions they corrupt to stay in power, but only how long they can keep them corrupted. They care only how far ahead they can push the impending disaster.

They prove themselves inferior in much that they do. Incapable of admitting embarrassment, they nevertheless fear that you will see them for what they are, laugh at them, and cast them away from their preferred place at the public trough.

Simple Wisdoms: Individuals and Society

Their ideas are bankrupt. Their view of democracy is to have one questionable vote used to justify more totalitarian control. Then they put their thumb on the scale for succeeding validation by election. Their view of free speech is to control what words are allowed that neither question nor offend them.

Their view of government removes checks and balances so courts can legislate, agencies rule by edict, and legislatures can be manipulated by party-selected leaders. Their view is that judges who used to call balls and strikes according to law cannot be challenged for legislating. Their view is that agencies should be weaponized to protect their rule, and that no punishment follows their overreach. Their view is that indoctrination is a necessary function of management. Their view is that military leadership, no longer bound by the chain of command, can ignore lawful orders from superiors and can politicize directives to undermine them.

Their view is that science follows policies set by officials, that credentials matter more than science, and that positions are validated by being official. Their view is that schooling matters more than education, that curricula set by credentialed officials is by definition sound, and that teachers, trained to teach rather than master subjects, need only push what is authorized from above. They believe that imposed equity matters more than excellence.

Their view is that the commercial middle class needs to be rubbed out, corrupted, or destroyed to give them free reign.

Their view is that language is political, so adjectives like "environmental," "restorative," and "social" can negate justice, "stakeholder" can undermine capitalism, and "civic" can mask the clarity of virtue. Their view is they can play superficial characteristics of "identity" politics off on others while claiming uniqueness through self-selected personal pronouns.

Their view is that they get to define your words for you, and that you should be punished if you object. Their view is that if they choose to take offense, what is becomes what is not, and what is not, becomes what is. Their view is that they can punish you for hate if you disagree. Their view is language that redefines common meanings of words weakens clear thinking in favor of top-down uniformity. They believe in America, but one they get to define.

Their view is that none of their increasing pile of lies will be challenged because schools already dull students, electronic media cow under regulatory threats, and corporate media follow along to preserve their oligopoly. They are content that broadcast media and the press generally transmit in one direction, naturally throttling any challenge to their word. What they pass off as news is preposterous, but their one-way channels preclude a *Mystery Science Theater 3000* backchannel of sarcasm and laughter.

Their view is that political parties are manageable through self-selected elites, that agencies can subvert the campaigns of those with whom they disapprove, and that ballot integrity, buried by judges and legislators, no longer matters.

Their view is that guaranteed income keeps urban voters in line without improving their quality of life, that centralized tax-paid healthcare keeps people beholden, and that health officials are authorized to bypass the Constitution to run or to ruin segments of the economy as they see fit. Their view is that a loss of personal responsibility is positive because it promotes a loss of civic engagement.

Their view is that it is proper to stampede crowds to undermine the lives of those who disagree with them, and that gun control is necessary for order rather than to save lives.

Their view is that national boundaries are an unnecessary obstacle to centralized global rule, and that immigration restrictions are no longer necessary. Their view is that prosecutors are just if they selectively treat crimes unjustly in the name of justice. Their view is punishment is the wrong answer for those they favor who commit crimes.

Those who so blatantly lie are no different than those who would pee on your shoes and tell you it's rain. Yet neither their associates, their political opposition, nor even the press you pay for call them out for statements that are obviously inconsistent, logically absurd, and at odds with the record of facts.

Their view is that they may collect as much in taxes as they want, and they are at liberty to use those tax dollars however they see fit, unbound by the Constitution, laws, elections, or the need to repay those debts. Their view is that society is theirs to mold by dictating social morés and new traditions regardless of history and heritage.

Purposely supplanted individuality

In the 50 years between the 1970s and today, the fiction then accentuates the extent today's reality has traveled. Cpl. Maxwell Q. Klinger, the deadpan crossdresser played by Jamie Farr in the 1972 *M*A*S*H* TV series, portrayed individuality with a purpose. Current toxic leftist bluster brazenly pushes facts it knows are not true, claiming policy to be an adequate substitute for reason. Officials undermine individuality by posturing to protect individuality as their policies throttle liberty, freedom, and common sense.

In order to escape the craziness of the Korean Conflict, Klinger donned a dress in hopes of gaming the Army into granting him a psychiatric discharge. As he carried out his daily duties, officers and enlisted troops treated Klinger as the individual he was.

Today's official Woke approach in the military goes beyond tolerate, beyond accept, and on to celebrate, insisting others cede their individuality to official policy or face punishment up to and including dismissal. Individuality is now the official talking point of total, authoritarian control. The military is one-agency, but a current Presidential Executive Order has appointed a "czar" to see that the policy will be pushed into every agency of the administration. Conformity is control.

So many things at one time are warped. Why do authorities believe they can get away with it? The answer is because they already have. They are not held accountable for what they do. Furthermore, what is wrong with culture and society is your fault, not theirs. For generations those hired to stand guard have failed, including the press and elected representatives. In part they failed because they were told to trust experts hired to set curricula, as if credentials indicated skill and knowledge, when the only real experts are those who can explain things so clearly even we can understand.

Where experts fail

Little across several generations of highly structured, subject-based academia — including Social Studies, Political Science, Sociology, History, Philosophy, and the like — seemed to prepare students to deal with the simple daily problems of living — such as how to recognize what matters in society.

That's understandable insofar as such classical thinking skills of deduction and detection of logical fallacies were replaced in the 1500s by teaching subjects with the hope students would magically learn to think. Modern Social Studies, fashioned by such progressive educationists as John Dewey in the early 1900s, emphasized school communal training more than it provoked reflection on the past. College Political Science called itself science but dealt mostly in "Little-t" truths that, while true, were too insignificant to be useful. School History fell back on testable events rather than the threads of wisdom to be gleaned from experience. Sociology, in its quest for neutrality, decided morality doesn't have a place in its views. Philosophy, like the Greek mythological ouroboros, swallowed its tail since the 1940s as it mused whether it could know anything at all rather than help people deal with the simple daily problems of living.

Academics, then, really didn't lose their way so much as they never mastered what Confucius 2500 years ago called *li* or "The Way." Having never figured out for themselves how to behave, and having to fill a 50-minute period each day, they improvised, unfortunately, with limited success.

In his 1850s book *Hard Times*, Charles Dickens pointed out their misguided ways. He chastised schools for teaching bare facts. Since then, teachers studied the lives of famous people in hopes of finding behavior to emulate. They pushed "core values" rather than refine the process of clear thought. They hung posters in praise of more than 200 different virtues, without explanation where such virtues came from or why such virtues matter. And yet, they seldom consider the minimal requirements of behavior at society's edge where any two individuals or any two groups meet.

Character isn't enough

No government can afford to be indifferent to the character of citizens, but we are no longer producing such citizens. Too often pushing character misses the mark. Character springs from fundamental principles that are personally deduced like humility, reciprocity, and one's sense of time and place in it. Character springs from the compelling logic of what you master. When you master logic, logic masters you. When you prove to your satisfaction that 2+2=4 and not 5, nothing will convince you otherwise.

Character is not about applying rules. It's about being able to make complex life decisions—and to understand, justify, and apply the solid foundation of process concepts that lead to character. For those unable to grasp the dynamics of ethical decision-making, Confucius' ritual and rule-based system of law helps one act honorably in society with others. Niccolò Machiavelli came to a similar conclusion writing, "a prudent individual knows many goods that do not have in themselves evident reasons with which one can persuade others."

Character represents the processes one mind uses to decide how to act toward others. On a practical level, it addresses "What can we know?"; "How should we act?"; and "How should one deal with others?"

Early philosophers did not have metaphors like recursion or refined words to write about themselves. Our challenge is to go beyond rewarding good behavior, which Kant recognized was ineffective, to do that which Socrates called not 'teachable, like geometry,' but teachable in a way, that we might produce not docile sheep but responsible, growing, inquiring citizens.

Aristotle could not express character, but his intellectual virtues encouraged character. Character is not about demonstrating virtues, but about validating the internal processes to deduce virtues. My wife explains, 'Well, I don't love to iron; I love to have things ironed.' The example differentiates between the process and the result. People love the result we call virtues much like they love pressed clothes. They don't care to do the slogging that will get clothes pressed. To them, admiring pressed clothes is quite enough to get them all pressed. That would sound like a joke if it weren't an accurate analogy. You can talk about something, want something, and not understand the thing you want.

At the beginning of the 20th century, Virginia Woolf's novels tried to represent how uncertain and complicated thinking and consciousness are. They did not advocate a process by which an individual could develop mastery of character in oneself or society. Woolf and James Joyce described consciousness at work. As Woolf represented consciousness, she did not address constructive use of consciousness. Their Modernism did not address how individuals gain their society. Consciousness is not character but the mechanism by which character can happen. Literature like Woolf's can describe your despair, but great literature should suggest a way out.

Developing character is a two-step process. First, stimulate the interest and ability to examine their own personal experience for useful lessons like humility, reciprocity, and the sense of time and one's place in it. Second, compare their lessons from their experience with your lessons from your experience to extract shared observations that could lead to a common framework for decision-making. Such is the way to create both character and society with others.

Civic virtue isn't enough

Where does the "civic virtue" that professors teach and authors promote come from? How is it different from any other virtue? And does a virtue ever stand on its own or always fall out of the process of thinking clearly?

If teaching virtues is what should be taught, then there should be a clear path to explain how one gets from the vocabulary to character. Instead, they propose to teach vocabulary, not judgment. The practice of teaching the vocabulary of virtue may not develop character by any means other than chance. It seems learning virtues is different than developing virtue. They think mastery of the vocabulary of virtues is character. Virtues to them are like numbers trying to substitute for mastery of arithmetic. "Seven! Seven is a good number! Learn seven and arithmetic will certainly follow. Five! Five is another worthwhile number. Master seven, five, and several more and arithmetic will magically appear."

The problem of how to teach character is very old. Socrates died for it in 399 B.C. when trying to wrest teaching from the government. In the 1700s, Immanuel Kant wondered why it was that moral instruction accomplishes so little. Yet, he observed, even little children understand that you should do a thing just because it is right.

Everyone deserves to be challenged why they should choose a character-centered life. Phrased better, that question really asks, why is such a life in one's own long-term best interest?

Why do people teach the result they want but not the skills to get there? Why should I be consistently moral? Why not be moral only when it pays to be moral? Why not be immoral if you can get away with it? Perhaps character education is only taught the way that it is because alternatives have not been clear.

Virtues are the result of thinking about yourself, society, life and your place in it. Our job is to seed that path with a handful of process concepts that people easily turn to help themselves. A virtue is a shorthand label for the result of thoughtful analysis about a general concept that is, itself, easily acceptable and easily understood from one's own personal experience. So many so-called virtues are able to be deduced from humility, reciprocity, and a sense of time. Process concepts like recursion — thinking about thinking — help people decide what to do so they can plan for their better future.

Humility, of course, maps to humility, but so does forgiveness. Benevolence, compassion, generosity, gentleness, tolerance, justice, loyalty, and others map to reciprocity and a sense of otherness. Responsibility, truthfulness, sensitivity, dependability, alertness, and sincerity all map to regard for the accuracy of one's mental map of reality.

People insist on trying to push character onto others when much of the real work—the work inside their own head— remains unfinished. American minds before the American Revolution were better tuned to the proper limits of government than Americans are today. George Washington's character mattered, because, as you master logic and logic masters you, character instills the courage to persevere. Today, not all American minds are prepared. If you think you know what to do but don't know why, then you don't know character or civic virtue, much less how to convey it to someone else.

The tools character promoters regularly choose to use — such as vocabulary and emulation — show lack of respect for voters and for society. If they understood what they were doing or if they cared, character would not let them use such tools.

Morality isn't enough

Most other animals are outside the framework of morality. Morality is purely a creation of thought. A seal that snips off the fins of a fish, leaving it a terrified, living, helpless toy to be batted around until boredom and hunger make it lunch, has no concept of good and evil. Good and evil don't exist in the world of seals and fish; life is simply the way things are.

No compelling reason in the laws of nature or mankind will irrefutably justify morality to any and all men. One who chooses to act by the laws of the lion need not even consent to listen to the arguments in favor of morality. He need not choose to heed anything but that which compels itself to be heard by the laws of nature, if even that.

People cannot be forced to join together under the protection of a moral umbrella; we can only encourage them to do so by presenting its advantages and encouraging them to develop the thought processes necessary to weigh them. Our own best interest demands we help as many as possible to become so thoughtful, they clearly understand such things. Our security depends upon it.

Protection under the moral umbrella is not so much explicitly subscribed to by an individual as it is rejected by an explicit act. The minimums of society that we have deduced from experience are few. Similar guidelines apply at the level of foreign states or governance: Restriction of the freedom of communication, such as muzzling free speech or press, or hostage taking amongst the diplomatic community casts one out from the umbrella's protection to put them at the mercy of the laws of nature.

By such action one opens oneself to any response in the arsenal of the laws of nature we may choose to take. He has chosen the battlefield, not us. We, in turn, are subject to the laws of nature in our response. We need not reply using the standard of the moral umbrella the offender has rejected, although we may choose to do so. Pacifists and military generals of quality understand that war is a nasty place to be and should be avoided, if possible. But those of us who understand morality reserve the right to protect themselves by any means necessary. And one might survive or both might die. Nature does not care.

Kurtz' monologue in *Apocalypse Now* is brilliant even though neither Francis Ford Coppola nor Marlon Brando may have understood the insight that one can be willing to temporarily set aside morality to fight those who undermine it. Morality is the creation of those who choose to live under its protective umbrella and, in so doing, lift themselves just a fraction above the law of the jungle lived by the animal kingdom. Those who by their actions choose to reject living under the umbrella's protection can have no expectation that morality will protect them when society turns around on them.

Do not underestimate the value of the umbrella. Robert Bolt's Thomas More explained in *A Man for All Seasons*:

> And when the last law was down, and the Devil
> turned 'round on you, where would you hide,
> Roper, the laws all being flat? This country is
> planted thick with laws, from coast to coast, Man's
> laws, not God's! And if you cut them down (and
> you're just the man to do it!), do you really think
> you could stand upright in the winds that would
> blow then? Yes, I'd give the Devil benefit of law,
> for my own safety's sake!

Morality is not abstract. It is integrally tied up with the immediate practical protection of one's own life. That is one's first concern. The proper concern of others are their lives.

The future safety of any individual is integrally tied up with convincing as many other people in the world as one can the value of living under a moral umbrella that is equitable and valuable for wellbeing, and by actions that decide under what conditions they will be treated. Our best interest is to encourage the kind of thoughtfulness to understand the ramifications of individual actions. Here is where fundamental principles come in because they are easier to teach.

Looking at society this way sets up a practical, culturally independent "friend or foe" detector to identify behavior that would undermine society. More to the point, and emphasizing humility, society is put at risk when doubt is replaced by certainty.

You can't know what is true. You can only discover if what is asserted as true does not match patterns of experience. Philosopher Karl Popper explained that science is not about deciding what is true, but about embracing a continuous process to identify and reject what is demonstrably false. Phrased another way, society is at risk without the freedom to say something someone may not care to hear. That said, the freedom to offend does not imply the necessity to do so, nor does it determine the form it might take.

Tools for thought

The 1930s mystery writer and medievalist Dorothy Sayers explained in a 1947 Oxford University lecture, *The Lost Tools of Learning*:

> For we let our young men and women go out
> unarmed, in a day when armor was never so
> necessary. By teaching them all to read, we have
> left them at the mercy of the printed word. By the
> invention of the film and the radio, we have made
> certain that no aversion to reading shall secure
> them from the incessant battery of words, words,
> words. They do not know what the words mean;
> they do not know how to ward them off or blunt
> their edge or fling them back; they are a prey to

words in their emotions instead of being the masters of them in their intellects.[2]

It's not that people can't think—of course, most can. Answers appear in their heads. It's that they haven't the habit—haven't the practice—to check their work. They'll say, 'I'm thinking now' and, of course they are, for a time, until the attention wanders, the wattage lowers, and the autopilot takes over.

Richard Mitchell was a college grammarian who dissected the casual approach to words of those on his campus in a newsletter, typeset by hand, titled, *The Underground Grammarian*. He nailed to the page the sloppy habits of casual thought that led us to a sorry state where we are no longer vigilant. If one person has mastered a metaphor and another has not, who's deeper in the fog? If one person values metaphors and another doesn't see the point of them, who is deeper in the fog?

In *Less Than Words Can Say*, Mitchell wrote:

Many of my students seem unable to express themselves in any language whatsoever. They aren't utterly mute, of course. They can say something about the weather. And give instructions about how to get to the post office. They are able to recite numerous slogans, especially from television commercials, and the lyrics of popular songs and recent–very recent– political campaigns. They are able to read traffic signs and many billboards and even some newspapers. They can claim certain emotions with regard to various teams and even individual athletes whose names they often know. They can spin more or less predictable reveries about the past, or the future, either in very simple concrete terms or in sentimental banalities or both. But they cannot pursue a process. They cannot say why

---

[2] https://www.thomasaquinas.edu/a-liberating-education/lost-tools-learning

evidence leads to a conclusion. They cannot find examples for analogies. They have never even heard of analogies. People in that condition don't think of themselves as being in that condition because they don't THINK of themselves. They honestly don't think at all.

Reading the past

Along the way, we forgot how to pull a community together, not just across distances, but over time as well. We don't recognize the golden threads that draw us all together. Footprints in the mind of a culture tell a fascinating story of the last century.

Novels document what representative thinkers, acting as scribes, chose to put down on paper. They tell us as much about the 20th century as Homer's *Iliad* and *Odyssey*, passed down by generations of oral mythic tradition, tell us of the classic Greek era. The *Iliad*, for instance, was a chronology of external events and much less an exercise of the mind like the *Odyssey*, written much later. Similarly, the last century of literature is illuminating for what it might have taught us and did not. Heavyweights like Henry James and Joseph Conrad, around the beginning of the 1900s, carrying forward to the election today, have been engaged as if society has been in a century-long slow-motion train wreck that has gone mostly unnoticed.

At the forefront of literature of his time, James' *The Art of Fiction* championed authors' liberty. James was looking for something else, and, with neither space nor time for him to ventilate, he left morality as an afterthought. As a sop for readers, at the very end, James suggests that good writers will always write moral fiction because good writers write according to their core values. With that throwaway remark, James granted the 20th century license to write pretty much anything. He diminished morality to be whatever an author says it is.

Morality in literature isn't a mandate, but over that last century, it has been a marvelous opportunity underused as an excellent vehicle. In *The Americans*, James juxtaposed new American ideals next to longstanding European traditions in a clash that forced people to look at how they relate to each other, but he did not nudge them towards how to act. He presented American traditions as fresh, open to challenge, rough, and occasionally embarrassing, and European tradition, rooted in feudal times, as beautiful, engaging, and rusting from within. James exposed the weaknesses of both but left readers no further instruction.

Golden threads do extend all the way back to the earliest thinkers, but many ostensibly educated people might not see the useful understanding in that literature—first, because they didn't read it for that understanding, and, second, because much of the literature missed significant insights about society.

What can we do?

There is no need to prospect for Natural Law. The term Natural Law is like the word gravity. Everyone knows what it is but no one can define it. By assuming people know what it is, it begs the question and, without a definition, it's impossible to revalidate it for yourself. If it were God's Law, the objection is that it has no basis on which to convince those whose religious upbringing may be different, or on those who profess no religious beliefs.

If not from personal experience, how else would one winnow from the chaff the principles that stand the test of time? How else would one make principles one's own? How else would one master principles so thoroughly that they become compelling—so compelling they become knowledge?

Decide what matters and why it matters. Study how many who seem to have good hearts have tried common approaches that seldom help. Find what might be done more effectively.

Nothing is more important now that, as Jacob Bronowski noted, science has put such power in the hands of anyone who cares to learn that an iron box will no longer protect your valuables nor an iron door protect your family. We are in a race that there is no guarantee civilization will win. Happily, civilization has a better chance today than ever before, because all it takes to inoculate individuals to defend themselves is to see things in a more useful way. All it took for villagers to see that the emperor had no clothes, was a change of mind.

Bottom-up governance versus top-down rule

From 27 B.C. to 180 A.D. the *Pax Romana* imposed the rule of authority that evolved into a rule of law never matched before or since. They kept the peace, in part, by training people to be good citizens. For Romans, a citizen was defined as a good person speaking well. A citizen who could speak effectively could influence others—armed, as Dorothy Sayers advised, and conscious, as Richard Mitchell demanded. Each individual was to be further defense against excess. It's time to return to that.

Historian Victor Davis Hanson explained the depth of current obstacles:

> We are faced with a strictly disciplined, no-nonsense revolutionary party, well known from history that aims to change the nation into something unrecognizable by most Americans. And it feels that it has now created the means to do it.[3]

By definition, socialism is anti-individual, anti-community, pro-collectivism, and pro-top-down rule.

There is no reason to surrender individuality to others, but that is what they would have us do. They argue red herrings, like the solution to civic violence is to disarm people. The problem isn't guns, it's people who have little to look forward to because the incentives to work to better one's life have been trashed, because the skills that help one to advance have been driven out of government schools, because re-validating why character matters isn't part of schooling or many homes, because close-knit families are subverted by institutions meant to supplant them, because politics and corporate media lost their way, and because authoritarians want to suppress the value of individuality and

---

[3] https://amgreatness.com/2023/01/15/the-manic-methods-of-mad-democrats/

excellence for their own selfish reasons. Guns? Guns and violence are drawn across the path of discussion to distract—a symptom, not a cause.

Michael Anton has pointed out the pathologies of the current regime, and also pointed out the need for a fundamental basis for a sound political order. The current dance among liberals and conservatives, left and right, secular and religious, and natural right has been unfulfilling, unreasonable, and unsuccessful. Anton writes:

> In sum, natural right is external to the prudent
> man's deliberation; it is what he discovers via his
> deliberation." For the lay among us, he explains,
> "At the most basic, commonsense level, that's all
> natural right is: the notion that we humans don't
> get to choose what right or wrong are. They exist,
> if not independently of us—they are inextricably
> bound to our nature—at least independent of our
> will. Our role is to determine what is right or
> wrong in a given circumstance, based on a
> standard we don't set, and then behave
> accordingly.[4]

This was the notion of so many who wove together our American Constitution, and nothing over which political thinkers of today should bicker. How people thought in the 1700s was, in part, controlled by the words and concepts they had available to them.

With more nuanced language, we can distinguish culture from the underlying society as easily as we can distinguish the multi-varied threads of the pile of a carpet from the underlying warp and weft of the minimum requirements for society that give a carpet cohesion and structure. Society is created at the edge where any two individuals or cultures meet and decide to act. Humility and reciprocity are the minimum requirements, the warp and weft, of society.

---

[4] https://amgreatness.com/2022/10/24/natural-right-and-historicism/

Our language lets us see more clearly than Socrates could. His notion was that if one looked at the society that mankind created, one could project backward to gain insight into the make-up of an individual. The single word available did not differentiate between culture and society, which led to notions about the individual that do not follow. But the converse, notions deduced about the individual, provide insight about society.

Structures within a society

Some argue that when one is born into society that already exists, one is obliged to follow society's rules. They claim you owe allegiance to the society that nurtured you, as they overlook that as a member, you are an active participant in that society and as responsible for its integrity as anyone else. From the earliest age, even before achieving the wisdom of seniority, individuals actively participate by engaging, learning, and questioning.

This is particularly important now insofar as socialists believe they can hijack the country from the people. Officials in government practice socialism by regulatory overreach in an attempt to take over the country before you become aware of what matters in society and what you risk giving away. Their so-called education is really indoctrination to develop their shared moral habits and beliefs that, because they are imposed, are effectively totalitarian.

This is contrary to *The Federalist* authors who proposed that government withdraw from forming character and educating citizens, and instead protect people and their property, allowing commercial enterprise to operate so long as personal property and individual liberty were protected. The *Federalist* authors proposed to separate economics and politics, the individual and citizen, the church and state.

Many of the founders believed that functional republics must encompass small territories. And yet, small town America is America. Even large cities consist of smaller neighborhoods whose interests can be masked by political activism taking advantage of political structure. They claim majority votes as validation for whatever policies they choose to implement.

Regulatory intrusion has consequences that often get overshadowed by the ostensible goal for the regulation. For instance, the America with Disabilities Act does help many citizens cope with their disabilities but can hinder different social benefits. Suppose that government mandates that after the initial broadcast of a public television program, succeeding broadcasts must be closed captioned before being re-run. Although a positive concept, lack of funding to caption the piece often censors all other views of the program anyone else might care to see. Such is the problem with top-down mandates as opposed to encouragement or recommendation.

As a society becomes operational, many subsidiary situations grow within it that operate according to special, more respective sets of rules. An example might be a professional football team. Another example that the political side of society will have to deal with are businesses and industries where people voluntarily join as employees if they agree to operate according to set rules.

Working with businesses formed in society, customers choose with whom they will do business. Large companies like Amazon provide variety while smaller companies may be more agile and flexible insofar as they can be local and personally attentive. Bigness isn't necessarily badness, unless it chooses to use its market dominance to control and, after more than 100 years since President Teddy Roosevelt, there is plenty of evidence that businesses still try. Rules to follow have grown over time, but one needs to be wary of the potential for public/private partnerships to warp regulation and for employees to impose themselves on business management.

To avoid capture

In the rough and tumble world of *Romeo and Juliet*, William Shakespeare has Juliet claim:

> What's in a name? that which we call a rose
> By Any Other Name would smell as sweet;

But the reverse is not true. Despite leftist postmodern attempts to redefine words and institutions, a flower so radically, forcefully changed from within no longer deserves to be called a rose.

The blossoms of organizations within society form grounds ripe for capture by those who would control us. Postmodernism is often used today because so many are ignorant how patently absurd it is. In 1871, Lewis Carroll, in *Through the Looking Glass*, made readers laugh when he wrote:

> "When I use a word," Humpty Dumpty said in rather a scornful tone, "it means just what I choose it to mean — neither more nor less."
>
> "The question is," said Alice, "whether you can make words mean so many different things."
>
> "The question is," said Humpty Dumpty, "which is to be master — that's all."

Progress claimed isn't always progress made. For instance, some who would usurp control invoke "DEI"—Diversity, Equity, and Inclusion— as a laudable goal while their use of words in practice mean the opposite of what is commonly understood: "Diversity" is used to narrow the list of acceptable candidates to a subset of superficial characteristics, "Equity" is used to undermine rewarding of meritocracy and excellence to treat some people more special than others, and "Inclusion" is used to exclude a wide variety of candidates whose characteristics do not fit the stubby little yardstick advocates would impose.

In this circumstance, if you disagree, you are "racist" because anyone who opposes them must be. They bury the language in organizational guidelines and aspirations because no one would oppose the common meaning of the words, only to use the landmine as an improvised explosive device when the time comes to undermine social realities with superficial racism, sexism, ableism, and other contrived systemic word games. Label these games for the control they oppose and do not play their game. "Woke" projects a utopian future as it promotes chaos that destroys any possibility of achieving it. As Ibram Kendi wrote, in *How to be an Anti-racist*:

The only remedy to past discrimination is present discrimination," "the only remedy to present discrimination is future discrimination," and "the only remedy to racist discrimination is antiracist discrimination.

Like every organization, so too every form of government can become tyrannical. In a democracy, being "bottom-up governance," the capacity to make individual decisions matters. Democracy assures the ability to call "bullshit" in front of an audience tuned to judge the accuracy of the argument. Brought to consciousness by the charge, individuals choose to laugh into submission one side or the other. And, in the end, the penalty for bullshit ought to be to be ignored.

A concept like Freedom of Speech enshrined in the Constitution and the Declaration of Independence isn't enough. The parchment only represents the principle behind it. Society depends on the liberty to laugh at any idea put forward by anyone else who chooses to speak. It is not law that protects the laughter, but simple good sense open to anyone who cares to work it out. For that third class of people Confucius labeled that cannot work principles out for themselves, then a 'friend-or-foe' indicator honed by fundamental principles should flash in warning.

To prepare for times of warning, a representative democracy and/or a republic, when supported by an education system that actually works, is able to put forward candidates with enough character to stand up to a misguided crowd long enough to educate them about what matters. But we are only just learning what matters and how to make it accessible to everyone so we can incorporate into Core classes such wisdom that students can discover and use to inoculate themselves.

And for those who don't see it or do it, Mother Nature will not care. But, we do—for ourselves and our children. Among the things that distinguish between ourselves and others of the plant and animal kingdom are the skill to communicate complex ideas to each other and the potential to project the ramifications of plans for the future. If we do not exercise these, we revert to the level of others in the world of nature—governed by the rules nature requires and nothing more. We have to be human or be no more than an animal.

Structures outside a society

A society that is organized and operational needs to address how to deal with those whose decisions may be different or even may run counter to the principles of their own society. Traditionally, outside areas formed into Westphalian states, although how they came into being and how they change rule may not conform to decision-making in society.

On the other side, globalists work for a One World-type internationalist model absent federalist checks and balances. Either way, the "Friend or Foe" indicators applicable at the edges of society still apply.

Some devious Westphalian states may work surreptitiously to undermine our society from within. Globalists most certainly will, as H.L. Mencken noted earlier, if you strip away the words from the policies, control and farming the population is their goal.

It is governance distributed at the lowest effective level, and voluntary cooperation above that, that leads to effectively managing conflict.

Conclusion

Now that we have scrubbed the walls, disinfected, and removed the nits …what have we learned that is general, practical, and compelling?

Is it Natural Law if wisdom springs from personal experience? Is it Character if backbone stiffens based on lessons from personal experience? Is it Civic Virtue if you do what you do because your value society with others? Is it Morality if you see advantage in constructing a process of peaceful problem resolution?

It doesn't much matter what it is labeled or how it comes to be, so long as its purpose is understood, its worth tested, and its practice mastered.

Simple Wisdoms: Individuals and Society

An assumption of *The Federalist* was that to be functional, a people must be relatively similar in manners, habits, and customs, but that is not necessarily the case. When a "messenger line" of principle takes hold, change of mind is not only possible, it is likely, creating a shared future.

As a Simple Wisdom, you are not only an individual, you are important to society. Each individual is necessarily at the center of a personal universe with a unique consciousness that can determine a path of action. Your long-term best interest and the best interest of the society you work with others to create will determine what paths of action to take. At every level of social interaction, lessons personally deduced about society with others inform us of the decency and civility to be found in our actions and the actions of others. The principles individually deduced at the outset of this written journey make up the "friend-or-foe" detector that guides informing character, civic virtue, and morality.

This does not demean character, civic virtue, nor morality but rather places them in the context of everyday decisions. This nudge to common sense is worth making your own. Stand up for yourself, for your family, and for those you know and respect.

To be straight-forward: You are on your own. You need others, but only those also willing to respect you. You have a responsibility to those in the past who made today possible, and to those in the future for whom you help clear away the weeds. You owe as much to succeeding generations as those who nurtured you gave to you. Begin now.

Italian Marxist philosopher Antonio Gramsci believed that America would not be conquered by war, but by a long march through its institutions. And so it has been over the last 50 years: public schools, colleges, churches, political parties, corporate media, accrediting bodies, financial institutions, government agencies, regulatory capture, prosecutors, the military, large corporations, overblown urban areas.

Top-down, authoritarian rule is destined to fail because consciousness is individual, self-checking, and humbly social.

Students who object to indoctrination will speak out at school boards. Colleges will lose applicants as candidates find that decent work, family, and an education can be found elsewhere. Churches that lose their mission will be replaced. Political parties will find donors turn to individual candidates.

Corporate media will find subscribers and advertisers go elsewhere. Accrediting bodies will be laughed at. Financial institutions will lose their base. The military will fail to meet recruitment goals. Government agencies will find themselves stymied by courts. Public prosecutors will lose elections or be removed. New small businesses will meet people's needs. Small cities will meet the needs of citizens.

When your local newspaper runs flawed national wire service news articles, let them know you see where they have failed. Shine light on your representatives and senators for their non-essential platitudes. At every turn you can make a difference.

Pay attention to simple things:

- Listen to what others say, watch what they do, and compare it with the rigorous frame of reference you build from experience and regularly review. Prune away what is demonstrably not true.
- Restore political representation that disappeared with party centralization and that has been built into the laws of the land, designed to remove power from voters.
- Reject specious attempts to divide us.
- Remember our founders believed good government able to peacefully resolve potential conflict is as important as that government be representative.
- Vigilantly call out regulatory capture to minimize it.
- Make political liars pay. Laugh at them to expose the media that tolerates such behavior.
- Broaden how you gather your news. Discard rip-and-read pseudo-journalists who play to gain audience share. Turn the channel or skip the gatekeepers altogether, along with so-called fact-checkers.
- Find joy in wisdom you have found through yourself and others. Feel proud of your growing understanding of what matters and why.

- Support governance at the lowest effective level. The function of government is to manage and mitigate the effects of factions that form.

- Work to keep decisions as local as possible to minimize the impact of those who would hijack business and government.

- Invest time, your most precious resource, to family and friends that matter to you.

- Recognize, as your world gets smaller and should you live long enough to be old and frail, it is this intellectual dance that will still make you smile.

It's past time to put up with rude. Pull off as many layers of the velvet glove as it takes to get the attention of those who consider others their doormats. They are the ones who have given up on themselves as individuals. They grasp at causes they don't validate as if simple assertion validates their own lives. They could do better, but won't.

The most significant threat our country has ever faced is the attempt to invert the structure of America to become, not bottom-up governance, but top-down rule.

Individual understanding, along with economic advantage, compels social cohesion. Once understood, principles become rock-solid and a wellspring of courage, purpose, liberty, and freedom.

About the author

Stephen B. Waters is owner and former publisher of the *Rome (NY) Daily Sentinel*, a 10,000-circulation small-town newspaper in the middle of New York State, owned by his family since 1864.

Stephen was the second child in a family of five children that grew up in Rome during the post-WWII peaceful interlude. Mom, Shirley, a multi-talented artist, advised, "Give children a safe environment, love them, and leave them alone!" Dad, George, in addition to being publisher, filled the basement with train sets, a shooting range, a wood and metal working shop, a photo darkroom, and room for arts and crafts. The attic was filled with bookshelves.

In 1964, at the age of 16, Stephen traveled to Australia for a year attending school in Sydney and Darwin as an American Field Service exchange student. Returning, he gave 30 speeches and still managed to graduate with his high school class.

He attended Colgate University, majoring in both History and Political Science, worked at the college radio station, and learned to program computers. He attended law school for two weeks.

In 1970, he joined IBM, Poughkeepsie, as a programmer for the Large Systems Design and Development group. Two years later he accepted a job in the Netherlands salvaging a computer center at the Faculty of Science and Mathematics in Nijmegen. In June of 1974, he returned to Rome and the family newspaper to stay a few months to help computerize the newsroom. He retired 46 years later as the fifth generation of the family to serve as publisher.

In 1984, Stephen was fortunate enough to marry Wendy Williams, a neighbor, news reporter, and eventually a teacher, instructional coach, and elementary school principal. They have two children, Brad, the 6th generation publisher, and Sarah; and two grandchildren, Bryce and Ayden.

Although never outstanding, Stephen has enjoyed old-time pick-up hockey, skeet and IDPA pistol shooting, reloading, gardening, sailing, skiing, and, of course, thinking about thinking. Philosophically, he never expected to be this old this soon.

Other books written by the author

Individuals, Journalism and Society

By Stephen B. Waters
ISBN-13: 978-0-9845258-0-5 (Paperback)
    Library of Congress Control Number: 2010904051
ISBN-13: 978-0-9845258-1-2 (Hardcover)
    Library of Congress Control Number: 2010905491

As accessible simple wisdoms empower people, character becomes easier to develop. New metaphors encourage processes kids understand, admire, and wish to emulate in a deeper way.

And none too soon. Journalism suffers from pervasive fog. Consciousness slips away. Schools lose traction. Character develops by chance. Politicians play games. Economists forget what works. History and philosophy drift. Scholarship loses perspective. Religion and tradition stall at cultural boundaries. Misbehavior threatens society's fragile fabric. Literature and language languish as destroyers march through civil institutions in a world made more dangerous by scientific progress. Fortunately, all it takes is a change of mind.

Take Back your News

By Stephen B. Waters
ISBN-13: 978-0-9845258-3-6 (Paperback)
ISBN-13: 978-0-9845258-4-3 (Hardcover)
    Library of Congress Control Number: 2018901883

Help reclaim trust in journalism. This book will help you see:
• How individuals, journalism, and society depend on each other. • How schooling can shortchange you,
• How to defend against noise in the media, and
• How to take back your news.

Individuals Journalism and Society:
Epilogue — Lessons Learned
Screenplay by Stephen B. Waters
ISBN-13: 978-0-9845258-9-8 (Paperback)
Library of Congress Control Number: ****

Nefarious people have joined in a new battle for your mind. They believe your individuality doesn't matter, that journalism serves them alone, and that society expects them to rule.

While most schooling leaves people defenseless against their words, this synthesis will help defend against their bold misuse of ideas.

**These books are available for purchase
from Amazon.com and from Lulu.com.**

www.ingramcontent.com/pod-product-compliance
Lightning Source LLC
Chambersburg PA
CBHW060654280326
41933CB00012B/2186